Yusai Fukuyama

TAMBOUR
WORK

LACIS PUBLICATIONS
BERKELEY, CALIFORNIA USA

DEDICATION
To my parents

ACKNOWLEDGMENT

I appreciate very much the help and encouragement that I received from: Mr Jeremy Pearson, Curator of Applied Art, Royal Albert Memorial Museum, Exeter, my teacher Mrs Elsie Luxton MBE and my colleague Mr Saikoh Takano without whose help this book would not have been finished.

Front cover illustration: *The Ladies Waldegrave* from a painting by Sir Joshua Reynolds, courtesy of the National Gallery of Scotland.

SUPPLIES:
Tambour needles, handles, tulle netting and threads can
be ordered through:
LACIS.com 3163 Adeline Street, Berkeley, CA 94703 USA

© Yusai Fukuyama 1987
Originally published by
Dryad Press Ltd. 1987

This edition first published 1997
Reprinted 2007

LACIS PUBLICATIONS
3163 Adeline Street
Berkeley, CA 94703
USA

ISBN 978-0-916896-88-1

Printed in the United States

Contents

Chapter Three   20 Japanese Designs

Preface

Chain stitch is one of the most universal forms of embroidery and crochet and it has a long and international history. This stitch is the basis of tambour work the roots of which go back many thousands of years to China, where exquisite work was done in silk thread.

Eventually this art found its way through India, Persia and Turkey into Europe.

My aim has been to give you a confident start to one of the most exciting traditional arts. I have tried to keep to a practical approach which should give you a firm structure on which to build later.

This volume contains practical information needed to recreate both traditional and contemporary tambour work.

Packed with ideas to suit various decorative uses, this book is ideal, not only for beginners, but also for the experienced needlewoman eager to master this traditional art.

Veil of embroidered and slightly drawn machine-made bobbin net, English (Nottingham), early nineteenth century. Photograph courtesy of Victoria and Albert Museum

CHAPTER ONE

Tambour Embroidery

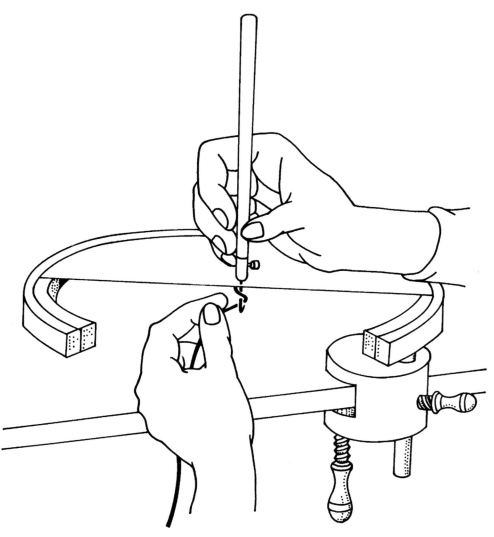

Tambour is a hand-embroidery technique worked by holding the fabric taut in a frame and using a hook needle to make a basic chain stitch.

The tambour hook is held in one hand above the frame, the other hand is positioned underneath to feed the thread onto the hook needle.

The right side of the fabric should be placed facing upwards.

The tambour holder must always be held straight in a vertical position; this allows for the easy movement of the hook in and out of the fabric.

If the holder is held slanting, like a pencil or pen, the needle will catch the threads of the fabric.

It is useful to remember that the notch in the needle below the ground fabric is directly aligned with the holding screw which remains above, therefore an indication of the exact position of the notch in the needle when below the fabric is available.

The length of the needle can vary from 8mm to 12mm.

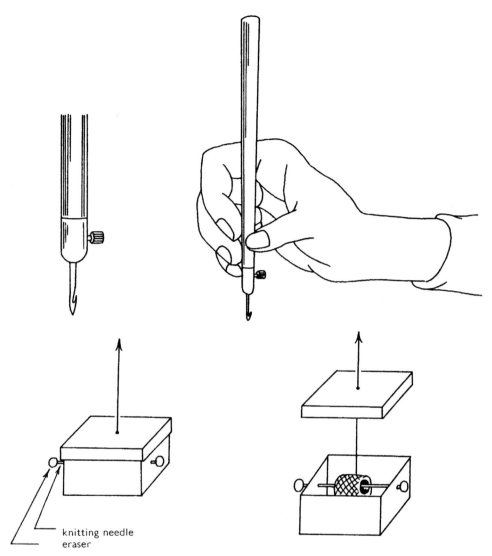

knitting needle
eraser

It is essential to work this type of embroidery in a frame with a stand as both hands need to be free, one to hold the hook, the other to hold the thread.

The thread must be placed in a position where it can run freely off the spool.

On the floor underneath the frame place a small box with a pierced lid to hold the thread.

To prevent the fabric from marking or slipping, you can bind the inner ring with tape before stretching the fabric.

1. Bind the inner ring with 2.5cm of woven tape (or bandage) and fasten with a few stitches.
2. To stretch the fabric, lay the area to be embroidered over the inner ring, press the outer ring over it.
3. Adjust the tension screw so that the fabric is smooth and the grain straight.

Equipment

Frames

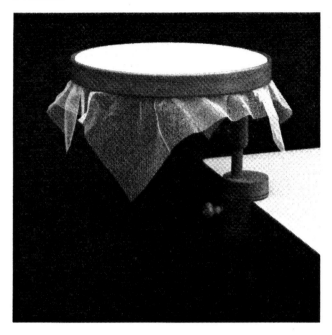

Ring frame with clamp

Ring frame with table stand

Rectangular frame with
table stand

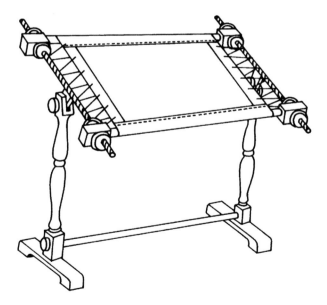

Rectangular frame with
floor stand

Ring frame and clamp

If you do not have an embroidery frame with a clamp or a table stand, you may use your ring frame as shown below.

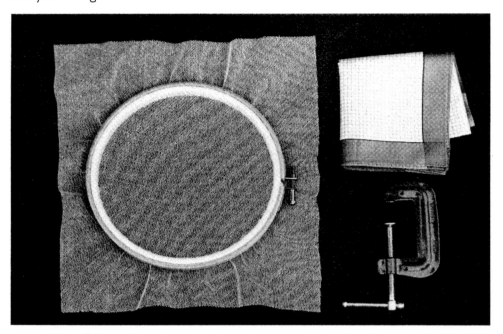

Ring frame with material and clamp in position, leaving both hands free for working

Thread

Many knitting, crochet and weaving yarns, raffia, macramé string, metallic and machine-sewing threads may be used.

Your choice of thread should be governed by your choice of fabric and the purpose of your finished embroidery.

An important point to consider is whether or not your embroidery will be home-laundered, dry-cleaned or displayed behind glass.

Embroidery threads are available in excellent ranges of fast dyed colours and textures such as:

Filo-Floss;
coton à broder;
pearl cotton;
six-stranded cotton;
linen thread;
soft embroidery cotton;
crewel wool;
and metallic threads.

Fabrics

Almost any fabric can be embroidered, from very fine silk and muslin to leather, felt and flannel.

You should choose a ground fabric suitable for the design and weight of the thread used, ie:

silk;
satin;
muslin;
evenweave cotton;
linen;
evenweave linen;
linen scrim;
hardanger;
felt;
and wool.

Needles

Needles (Schmetz) from the top No. 70, No. 80, No. 90, No. 100, No. 110, No. 120 and No. 130

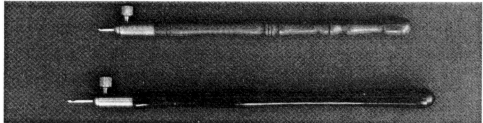

Tambour holders with needle

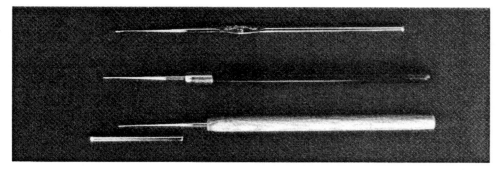

Crochet hooks

THE BASIC STITCH

Draw the design onto the material with a water-erasable fabric-marker.

Place a section in the frame, pulling it taut.

Do not knot the threads, but leave the ends hanging on the wrong side and sew down onto the back of the stitching when finished.

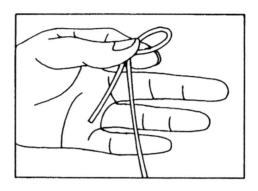

The thread is held in the left hand underneath the frame. Start at one side of the design

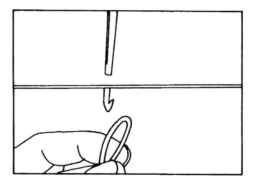

Insert the hook through the material to the back of the frame

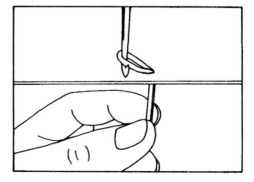

Catch the thread on the hook, and, leaving a 10cm tail, bring it through to the front

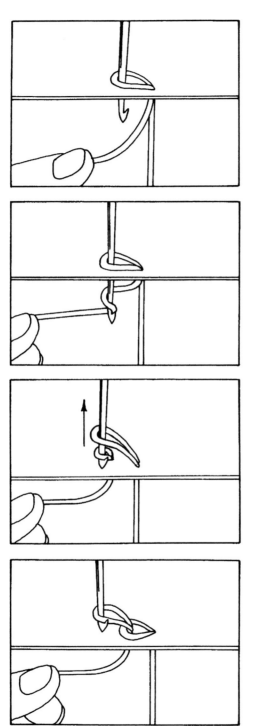

Insert the hook a short distance ahead and on the stitch line

Draw through another loop. Put a little pressure onto the smooth back of the hook. This avoids the hook itself snagging the fabric when it is retrieved

Bring the hook up to the top of the fabric while keeping the slight pushing pressure to the left

Draw the second loop through the first to form a chain stitch and continue. Make the loop slightly longer than the stitch required to prevent puckering

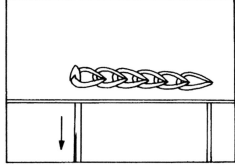

When the design is completed, disengage the hook.

Insert the hook from the back and pull the last loop through to the back

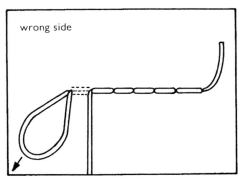

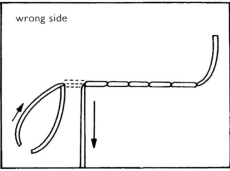

Cut off the thread, leaving a tail long enough to tie and neaten off

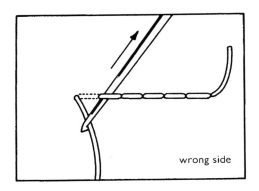

Using a hook

Weave into the back of the stitching with a hook or needle

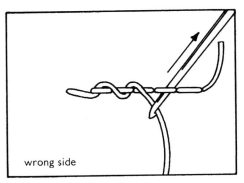

SECURING THE START AND FINISH OF THE WORK

It is advisable to secure the start and finish of the work very firmly, otherwise if the ends work loose the entire embroidery will come undone.

Take care not to tighten the thread when sewing as chain stitch puckers easily.

Using a needle

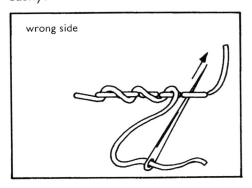

MAKING A SHARPLY-ANGLED POINT OR CORNER

Insert the hook from the back and pull the last loop through to the back

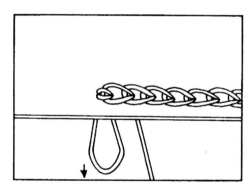

Make the loop big enough to allow the spool to pass through

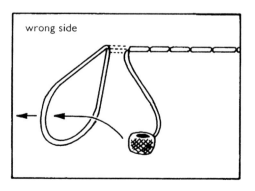

wrong side

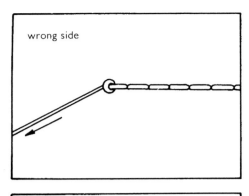

wrong side

Pull the thread gently; this makes a knot

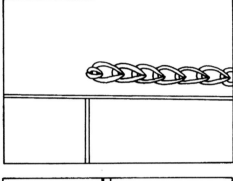

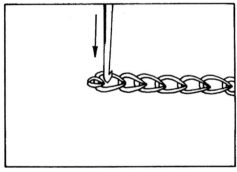

Insert the hook through the material to the back of the frame

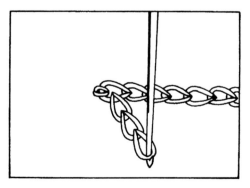

Each subsequent stitch continues to be worked through the previous link

MOVING FROM ONE PART TO ANOTHER

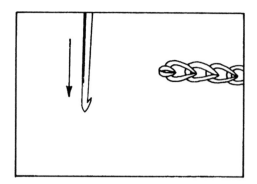

Insert the hook through the material to
the back of the frame

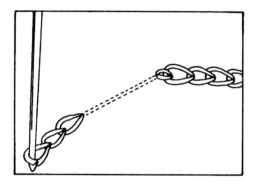

Catch the thread on the hook, and make
the stitches on the line of the design

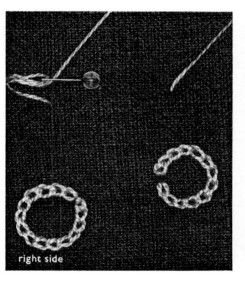

right side

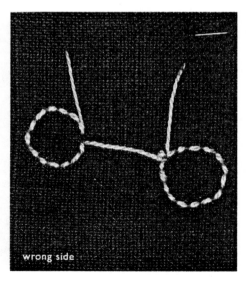

wrong side

DRAWING THE DESIGN ONTO THE MATERIAL

Draw the design onto the material (fabric or net) with a water-erasable fabric-marker or dressmaker's carbon paper. It is important that the loops making the outline are the same distance apart and that the threads making the loops are always of even tension. To fill in a motif, or to make all-over design, work the rows of the stitches close together.

I LEAF(I)

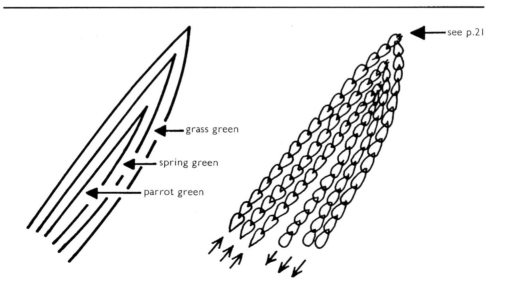

grass green

spring green

parrot green

see p.21

24

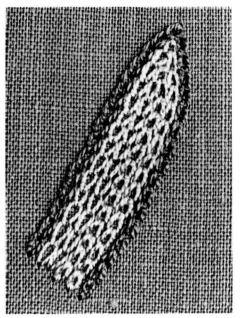
right side

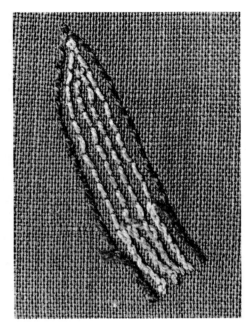
wrong side

2 LEAF(2)

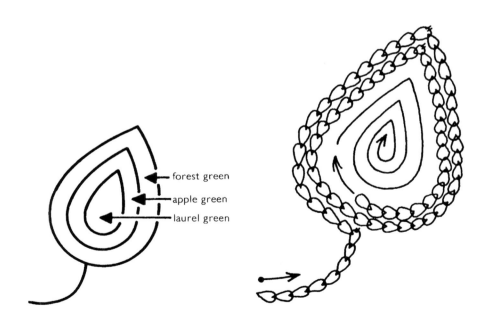

forest green

apple green

laurel green

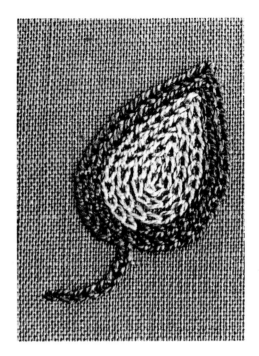

3 LEAF(3)

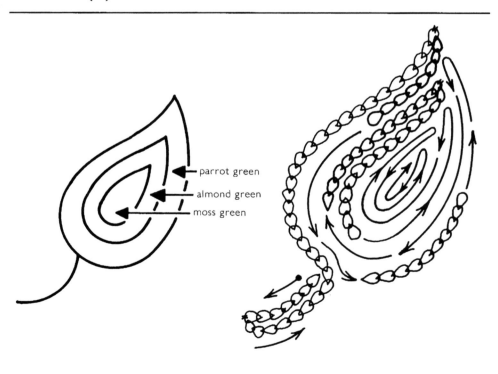

parrot green

almond green

moss green

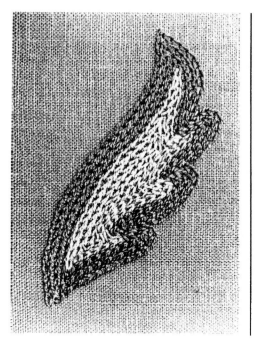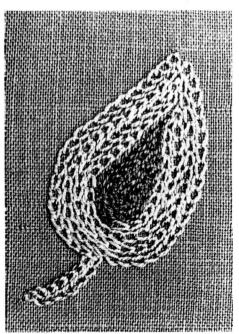

4 LEAF(4)

muscat green

moss green

moss green

5 LEAF(5)

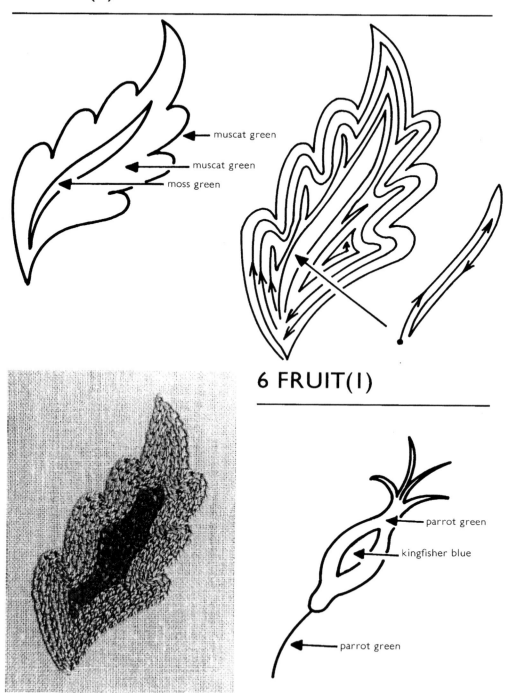

muscat green

muscat green

moss green

6 FRUIT(1)

parrot green

kingfisher blue

parrot green

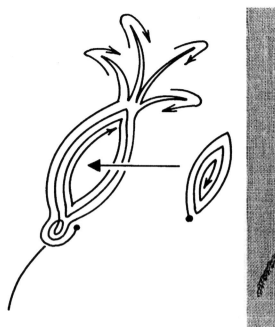

7 LEAF(6)

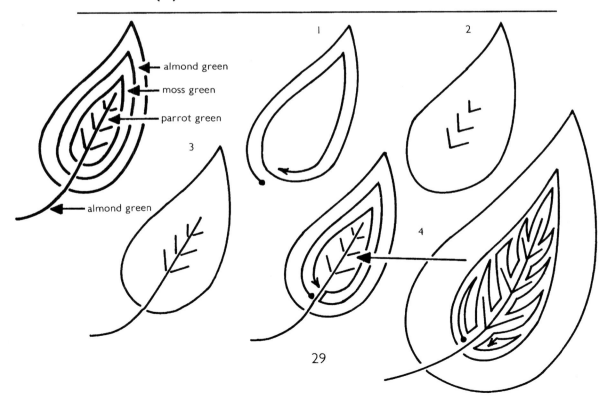

almond green

moss green

parrot green

almond green

1

2

3

4

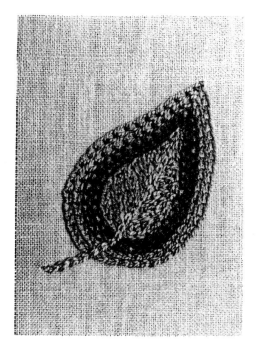

8 FRUIT(2)

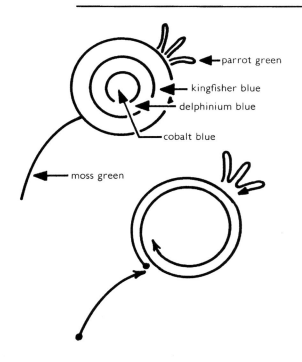

parrot green

kingfisher blue

delphinium blue

cobalt blue

moss green

9 FRUIT(3)

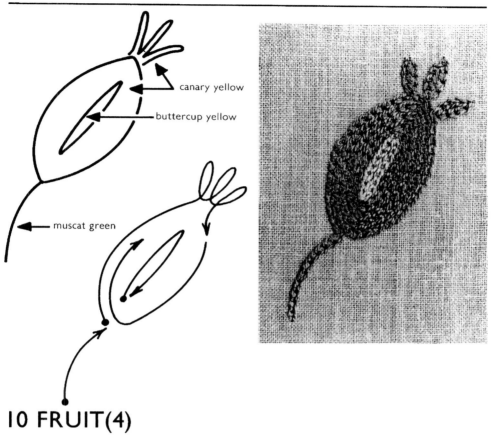

canary yellow

buttercup yellow

muscat green

10 FRUIT(4)

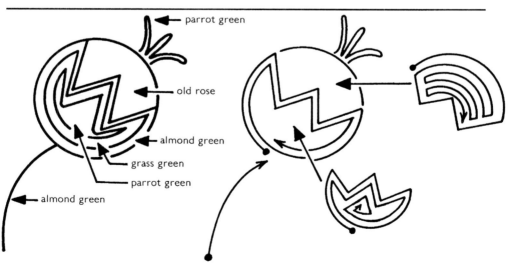

parrot green

old rose

almond green

grass green

parrot green

almond green

11 FRUITS(5)

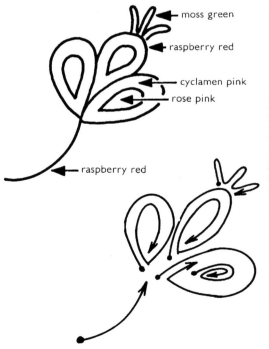

moss green

raspberry red

cyclamen pink

rose pink

raspberry red

12 FRUIT(6)

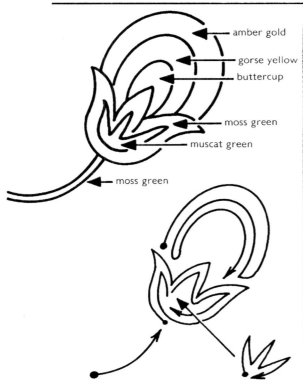

- amber gold
- gorse yellow
- buttercup
- moss green
- muscat green
- moss green

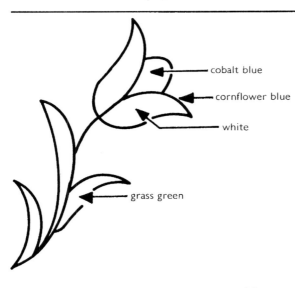

13 FLOWER(1)

- cobalt blue
- cornflower blue
- white
- grass green

14 FLOWER(2)

delphinium blue

cobalt blue

buttercup yellow

34

15 FLOWER(3)

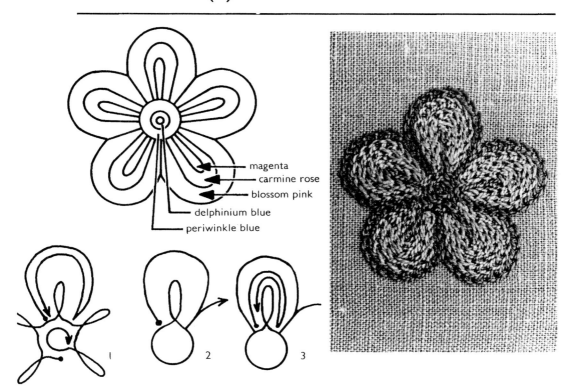

- magenta
- carmine rose
- blossom pink
- delphinium blue
- periwinkle blue

16 FLOWER(4)

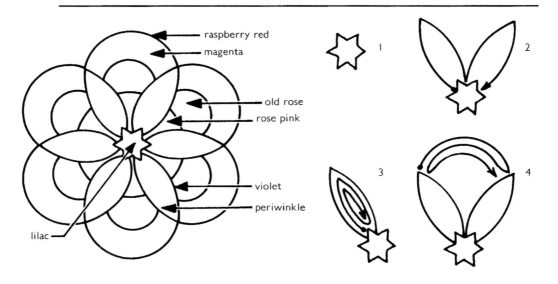

- raspberry red
- magenta
- old rose
- rose pink
- violet
- periwinkle
- lilac

17 FLOWER(5)

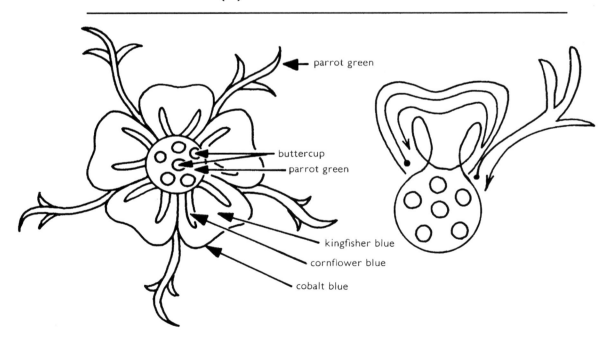

parrot green

buttercup
parrot green

kingfisher blue

cornflower blue

cobalt blue

18 FLOWER(6)

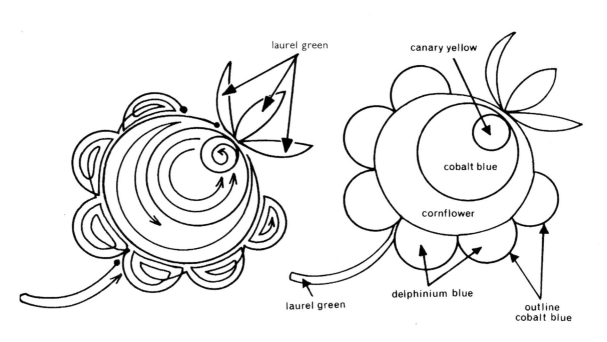

laurel green

canary yellow

cobalt blue

cornflower

laurel green

delphinium blue

outline
cobalt blue

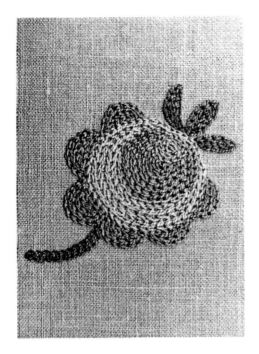

19 FLOWER(7)

22 FLOWER(10)

23 FLORAL MAT

COUCHING WITH TAMBOUR STITCHES

The coarse thread is laid down on the right side (top) of the fabric and stitched into position with another finer thread. It is then brought to the surface and worked along the design line.

When the line of stitches is completed the laid thread is taken through to the back of the work and secured.

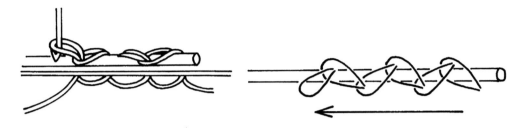

24 CORAL (I)

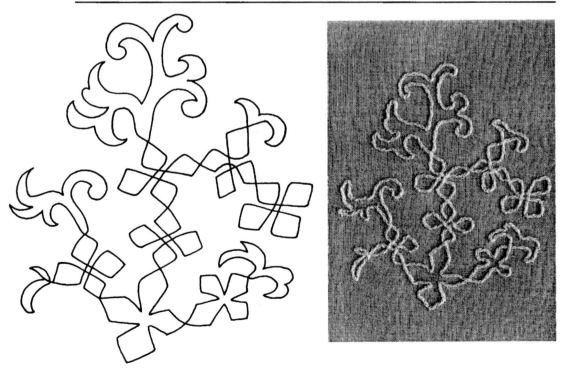

APPLYING BEADS WITH A TAMBOUR HOOK OR A FINE CROCHET HOOK

Trace the design onto the wrong side of the fabric. Stretch the fabric in a frame right-side down.

The beads are attached to the fabric from underneath.

Push the hook down through the fabric, picking up the beginning of the thread.

A loop is then drawn up through the fabric and the first bead pushed up to rest below the fabric.

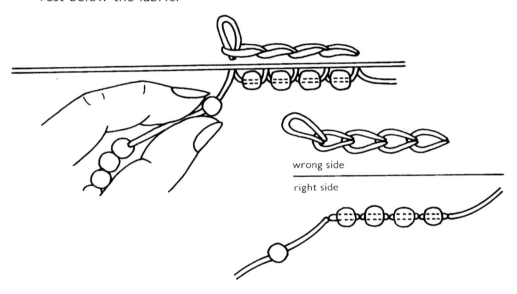

wrong side

right side

45

25 FRUIT(7)

 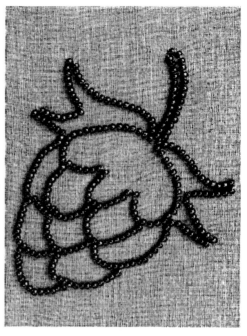

26 CORAL(2)

 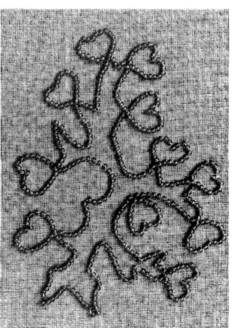

46

27 SUN ROSE

28 CAMELLIA

29 MOUNTAIN LAUREL

48

APPLYING SEQUINS WITH A TAMBOUR HOOK OR A FINE CROCHET HOOK

Method I

Trace the design onto the wrong side of fabric. Stretch the fabric rightside-down in a frame. Secure a long thread to the wrong side. Holding the sequins underneath, insert a fine tambour hook or a crochet hook half a sequin length away and pull the thread through to form a loop.

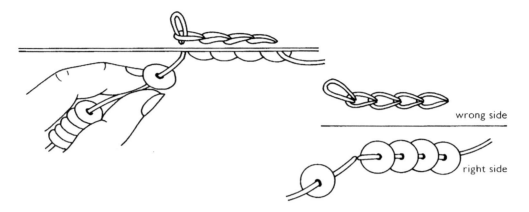

wrong side

right side

30 JAPANESE ARALIA

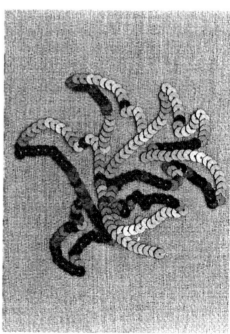

49

31 ROCK ROSE

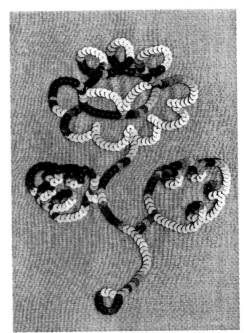

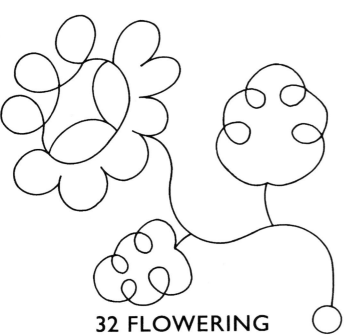

32 FLOWERING APPLE

APPLYING SEQUINS WITH A TAMBOUR HOOK OR A FINE CROCHET HOOK

Method 2

Trace the design onto the right side of the fabric. Stretch the fabric rightside-up in a frame. Hold the sequins on a fine tambour hook or a crochet hook and make a chain stitch.

This method is widely used in Pakistan.

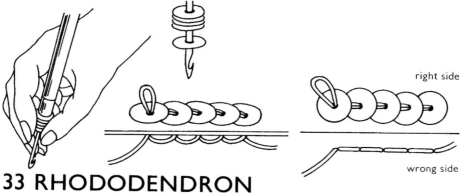

right side

wrong side

33 RHODODENDRON

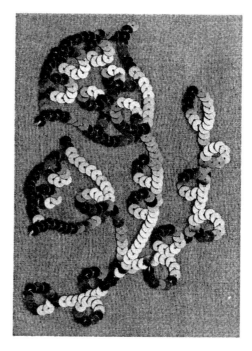

Wedding dress, English, 1911. Photograph courtesy of Victoria and Albert Museum

CHAPTER TWO
Tambour Lace

EQUIPMENT

Tools

Fine crochet hook (0.60mm) or tambour hook
Needle
Scissors

Embroidery frame

Use an embroidery hoop or a tapestry frame, but with an embroidery hoop always bind the rim with a soft material.

Fabric

Any fabric with mesh wide enough to allow the hook to pass through without breaking the threads will be satisfactory.

Thread

DMC Cordonnet Special No. 70 (below left)
DMC Broder Machine, Retors d'Alsace No. 50 (right)

Net

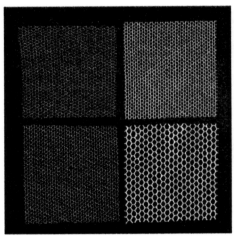

Silk net   Cotton net
Nylon net   Cotton net

FIXING THE END OF THE THREAD

The thread is held in the left hand underneath the frame. The free end is held in place between the thumb and the first finger

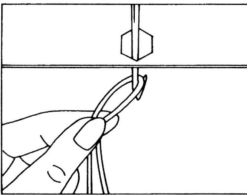

Catch the thread on the hook . . .

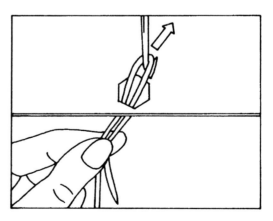

. . . and pick up a loop through the fabric

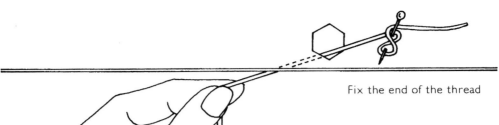

Fix the end of the thread

THE BASIC STITCH

Draw the design onto the material with a water-erasable fabric-marker. Place a section in the frame, pulling it taut. It is important that the loops making the outline are the same distance apart and that the threads making the loops are always of even tension.

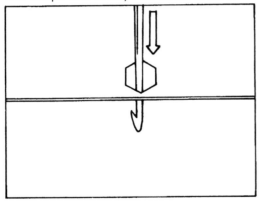

Starting at one side of the design insert the hook down through the hole in the net

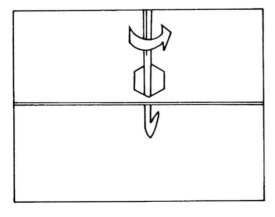

Twist the handle round between the thumb and first finger through 180 degrees

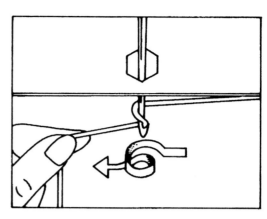

Wind the thread around the hook $1\frac{1}{2}$ times with the left hand (then hold the thread with the left hand in the direction of progress)

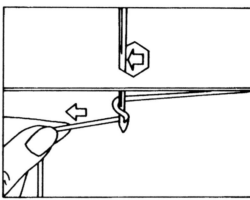

Keeping the handle upright, press the smooth side of the hook onto the front of the hole in the net. This avoids the hook itself snagging the net when it is retrieved

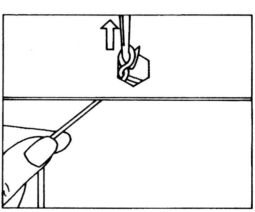

Pull the hook with looped thread through the net to the surface

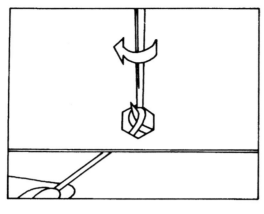

Twist the handle back to the original forward position

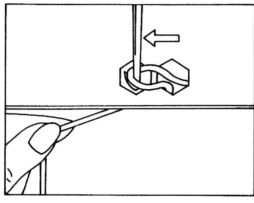

Insert the hook down through the next hole in the net

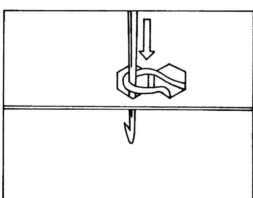

Twist the handle round between the
thumb and first finger through 180
degrees

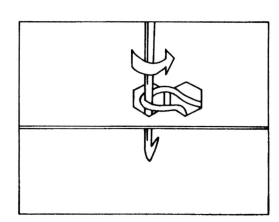

Wind the thread around the hook $1\frac{1}{2}$
times with the left hand (then hold the
thread with the left hand in the
direction of progress)

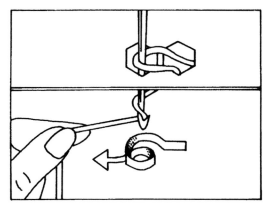

Keeping the handle upright, press the
smooth side of the hook onto the front
of the hole in the net

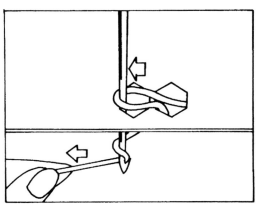

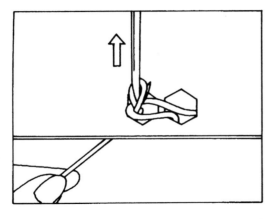

Draw the second loop through the first to form a chain stitch and continue

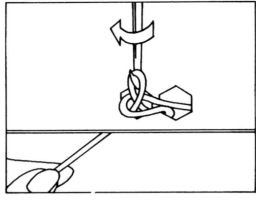

Twist the handle back to the original forward position

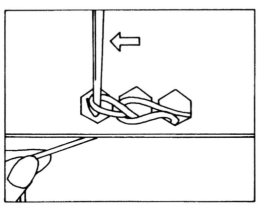

Make the loop slightly longer than the stitch required to prevent puckering.
   Continue in this way until the work is finished

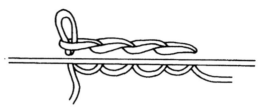

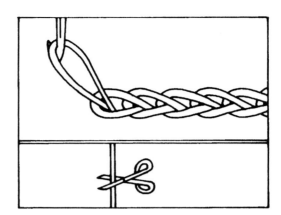

Pick up the last loop through the net
and cut the thread under the net

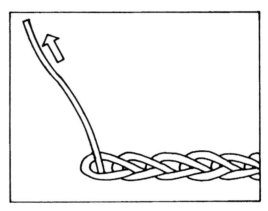

Pick up the end of the thread through
the net

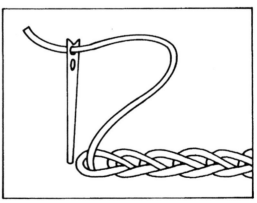

Do this using a needle.
 An easy-threading one is useful

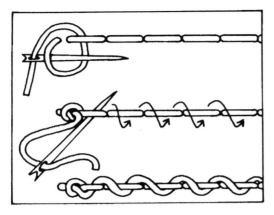

On the wrong side, sew into the back of the stitching

SECURING THE START AND FINISH OF THE WORK

It is advisable to secure the start and finish of the work very firmly. If the ends work loose, the entire lace will unravel.

Take care not to tighten the thread too much as chain stitch puckers easily.

Finishing

When finishing your work, bind the edge with chain stitch, using the same thread. Then oversew with fine thread and cut off any surplus material.

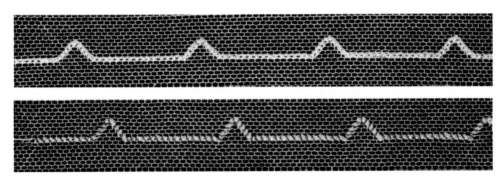

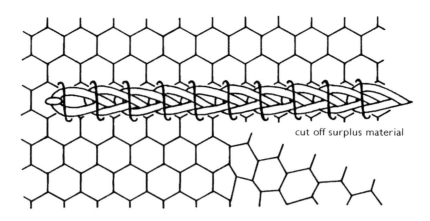

cut off surplus material

34 BROOCH PATTERN

35 BOOKMARK(1) 36 BOOKMARK(2)

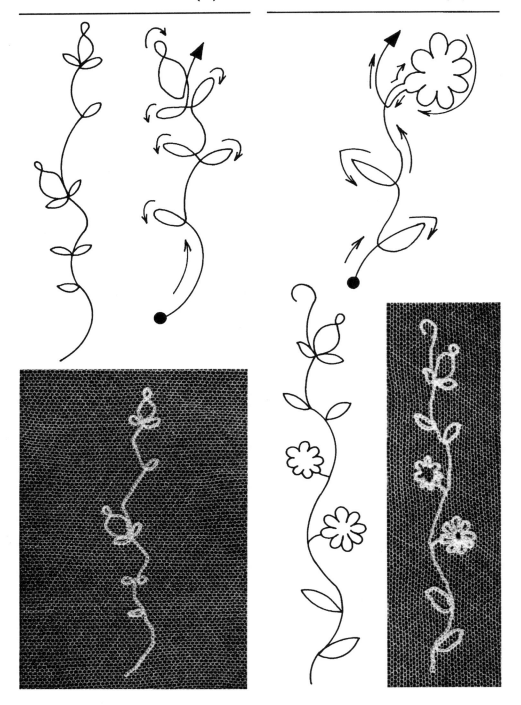

37 BOOKMARK(3)   38 PAPERWEIGHT(1)

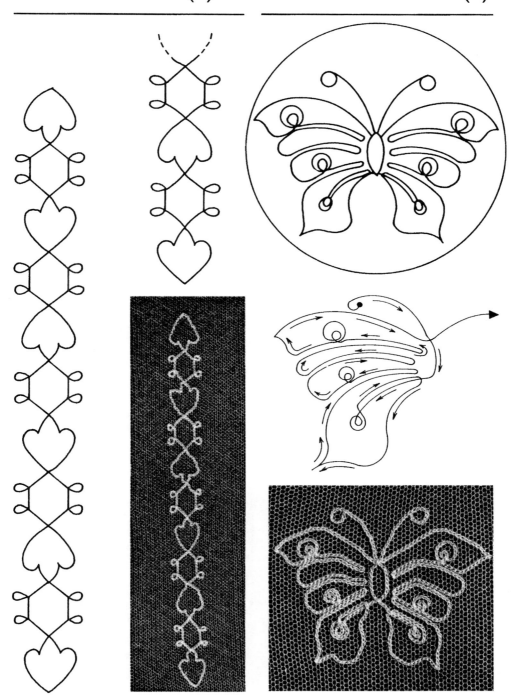

40 POT-POURRI SACHET(1)

Materials

Cotton net
Coarse thread: DMC Cordonnet Special No. 70
Fine thread: DMC Broder Machine Retors d'Alsace No. 50

41 POT-POURRI SACHET(2)

← centre

69

43 ROSE(1)

44 ROSE(2)

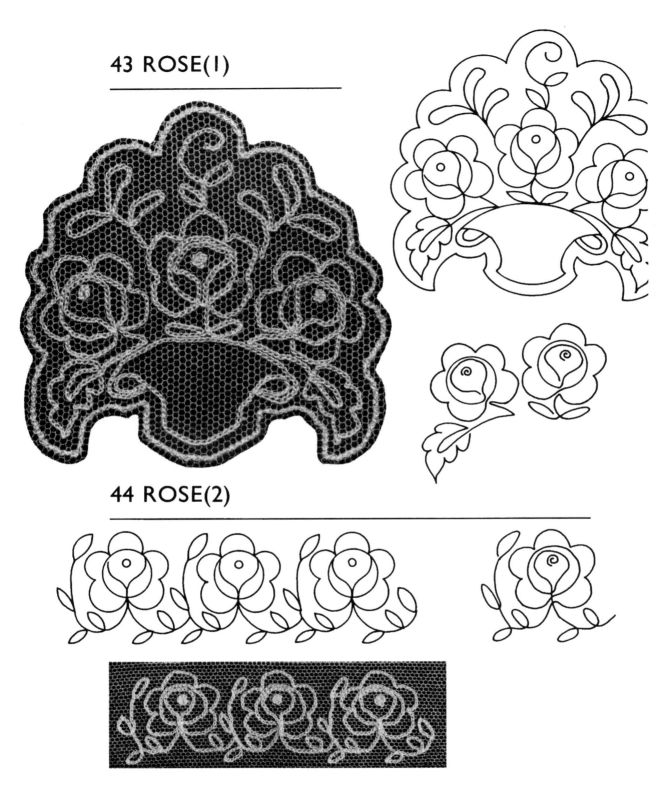

45 ROSE(3)

46 SCALLOPED
ROUND MAT

47 ROUND MAT

49 IKOMA

75

50 MIKASA

51 DAIGO

52 KIFUNE

53 VICTORIA

Materials

Cotton net
Coarse thread: DMC Cordonnet Special No. 70
Fine thread: DMC Broder Machine, Retors d'Alsace No. 50
(To fill in a motif and for finishing refer to p.59)

54 COLLAR (ROSE)

Materials

Cotton net
Coarse thread: DMC Cordonnet Special No. 70
Fine thread: DMC Broder Machine, Retors d'Alsace No. 50 for finishing (refer to p.59)

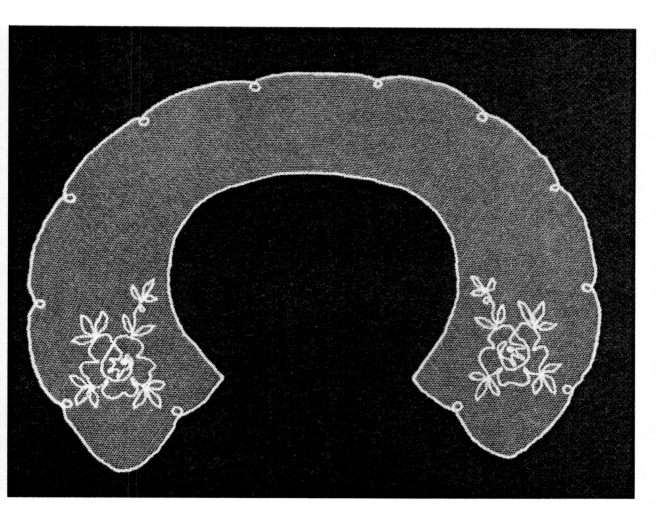

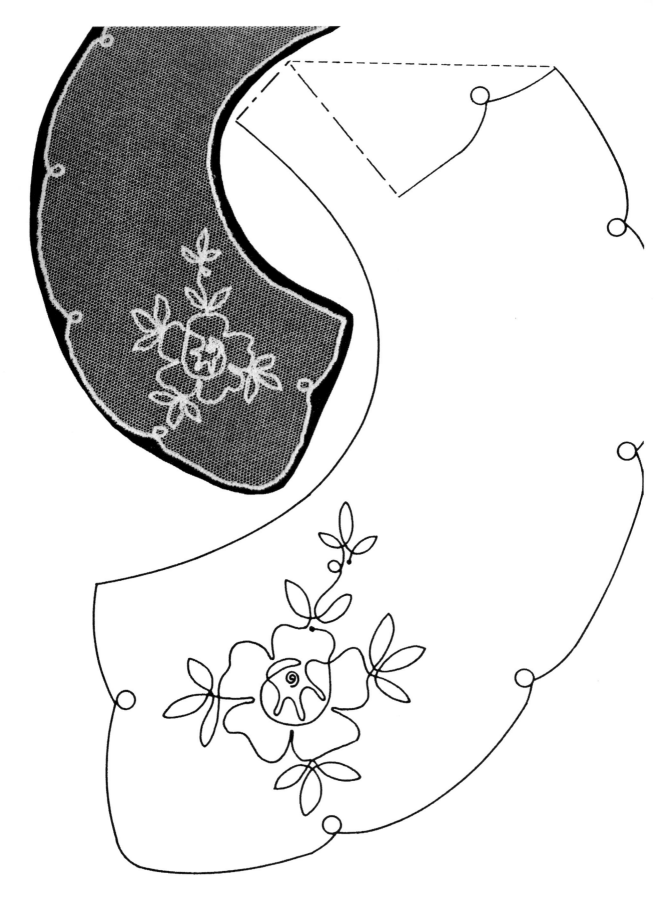

55 COLLAR

Materials

Cotton net
Coarse thread: DMC Cordonnet Special No. 70
Fine thread: DMC Broder Machine, Retors d'Alsace No. 50 for finishing (refer to p.59)

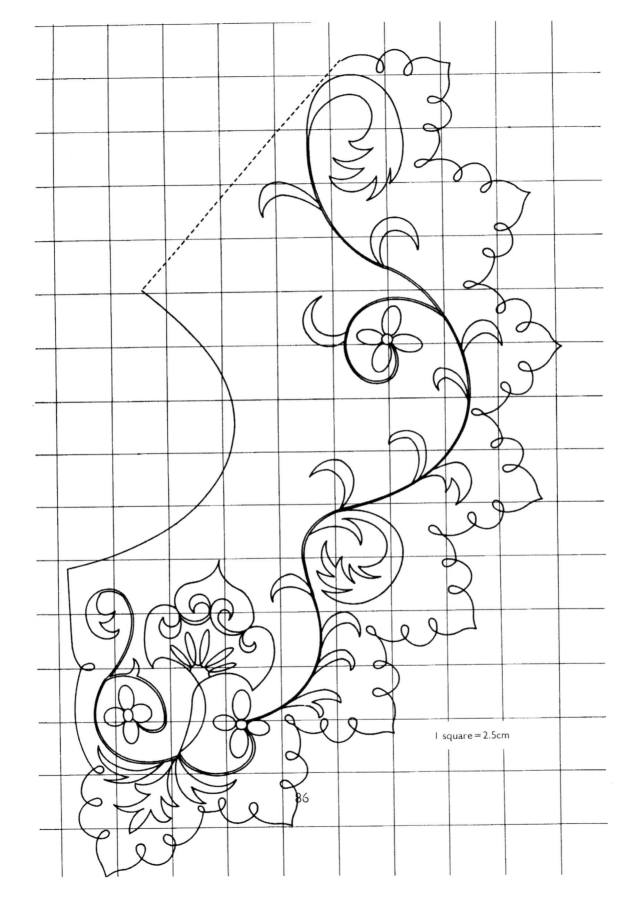

I square = 2.5cm

86

56 UJI

Materials

Nylon net
Coarse thread: DMC Cordonnet Special No. 70
Fine thread: DMC Broder Machine, Retors d'Alsace No. 50

57 ASUKA

Materials

silk net
silk thread

88

58 ROSE (4)

Materials

Cotton net
Embroidery thread No. 25
(two of the six strands)

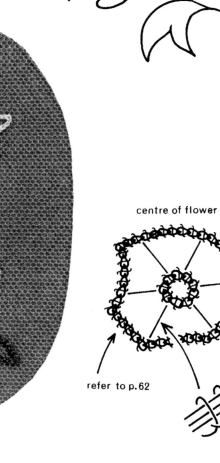

centre of flower

refer to p.62

59 KASUGA

Materials

nylon net
gold thread

Wedding dress, English, 1848. Photograph courtesy of Victoria and Albert Museum

CHAPTER THREE

20 Japanese Designs

MOUNTING SMALL PIECES OF NET

The pieces have to be attached to a supporting fabric.
1. Sew the piece onto a larger supporting fabric.
2. From the wrong side cut away the supporting fabric inside the square.
3. Place a section in the frame, pull it taut.
Tambour stitch is worked in a continuous line.

Materials

Thread: DMC Cordonnet Special No. 70
Hook: Tambour hook or fine crochet hook (0.60mm)
Net: Fine cotton net

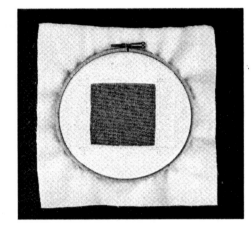

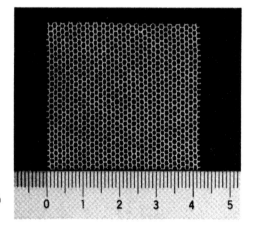

(cm)

61 ORIENTAL FLOWER

62 CRANE(1)

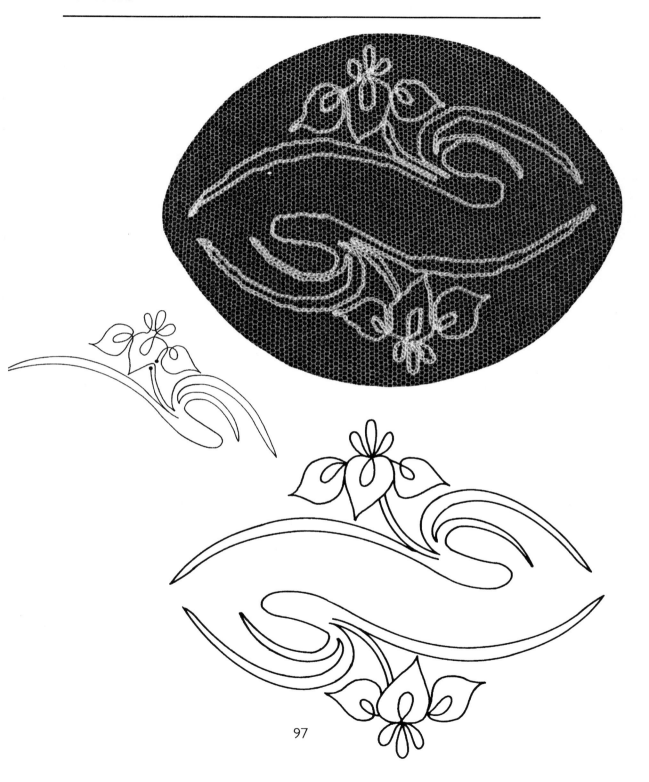

64 PLUM TREE

65 FERN

66 PEONY

67 PAULOWNIA(I)

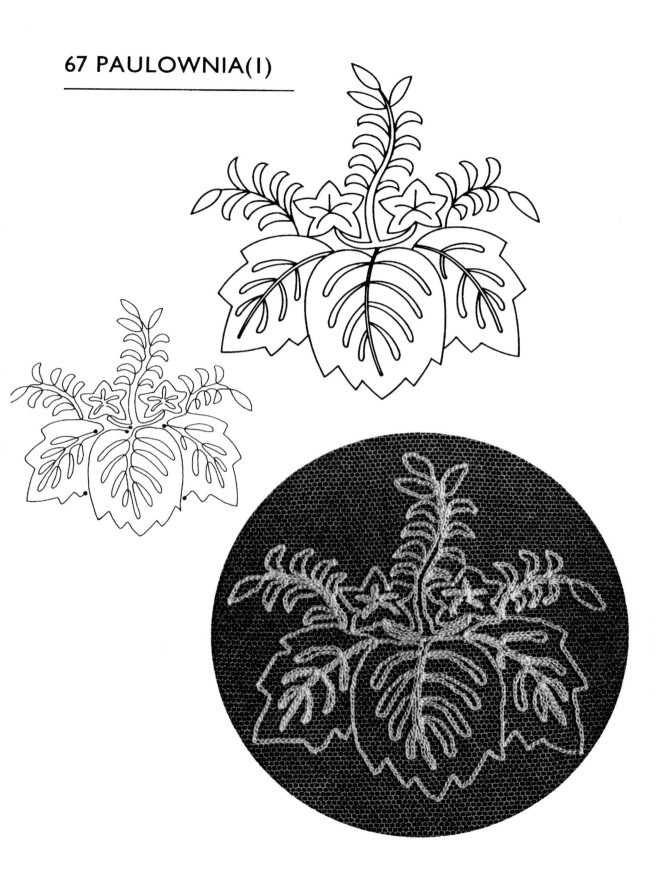

70 GENJI
BUTTERFLY

71 DRAGONS

72 SNOWFLAKE(1)

73 SNOWFLAKE(2)

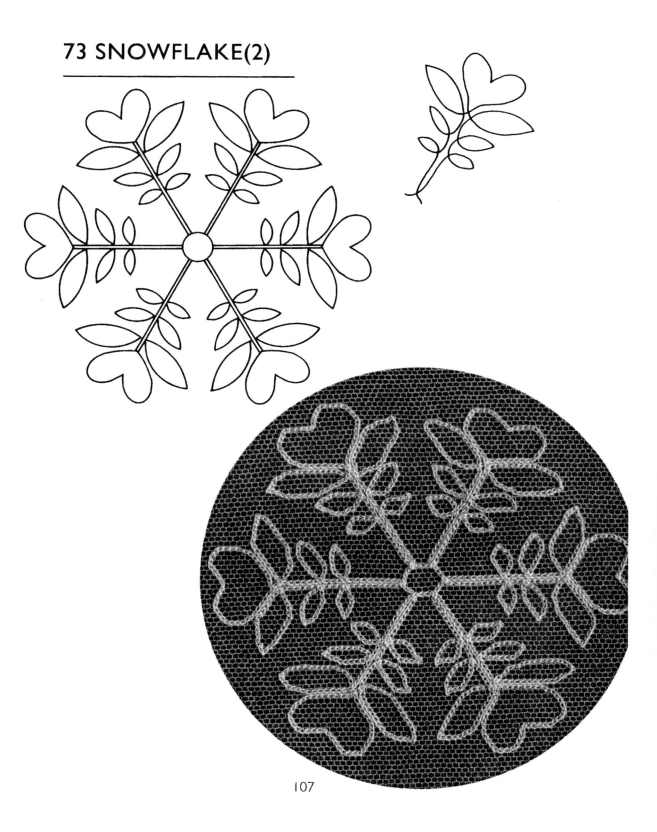

74 WISTARIA

75 KORIN
PAULOWNIA

76 CRANE(2)

77 CHIDORI
(PLOVER)

78 KASUGA

79 JAPANESE BUTTERFLY

Bibliography

Anchor Manual of Needlework, B T Batsford Ltd, 1958

Beaney, Jan, *Stitches: New Approaches*, B T Batsford Ltd, 1986

Best, Lugg and Tucker, *Needlework School*, Windward, 1984

Brittain, Judy, *Step-by-step Encyclopaedia of Needlecraft*, Ebury Press, 1979

D'Arcy, Eithne, *Irish Crochet Lace*, Dolmen Press/Dryad Press Ltd, 1985

Dudding, Jean, *Creating Coggshall Lace*, Jean Dudding, 1979

Edwards, Joan, *Bead Embroidery*, Lacis, 1992

Groves, Edna, *A New Approach to Embroidered Net*, Dryad Press Ltd, 1987

Houston-Almqvist, Jane, *Celtic Embroidery*, Dolmen Press/Dryad Press Ltd, 1985

Houston-Almqvist, Jane, *Mountmellick Work: Irish White Embroidery*, Dolmen Press/Dryad Press Ltd 1985

Jarratt, Maisie, *Embroidery Beading Designs and Techniques*, Kangaroo Press, 1992

Jarratt, Maisie, *Embroidery Beading with Australian Flowers and Birds*, Kangaroo Press, 1994

Jarratt, Maisie, *French Embroidery Beading, How to Bead*, Kangaroo Press, 1991

Jarratt, Maisie, *Tambour Beading with a Ring Frame*, Kangaroo Press, 1994

Johnson, Beryl, *Advanced Embroidery Techniques*, B T Batsford Ltd 1983

Jones, Julia, *Beading Book*, Lacis, 1993

Littlejohn, Jean, *Fabrics for Embroidery*, B T Batsford Ltd, 1986

O'Cleirigh, Nellie and Rowe, Veronica, *Limerick Lace*, Colin Smythe, 1995

O'Connor, Eileen, *Irish Lace Making*, Dryad Press Ltd, 1973

Palliser, Mrs Bury, *A History of Lace*, E.P. Publishing Ltd, 1902

Snook, Barbara, *Embroidery Stitches*, Dryad Press Ltd, 1985

Thompson, Angela, *Embroidery with Beads*, Lacis, 1992

White, Palmer, *Haute Couture Embroidery, The Art of Lesage*, Lacis, 1994

Index